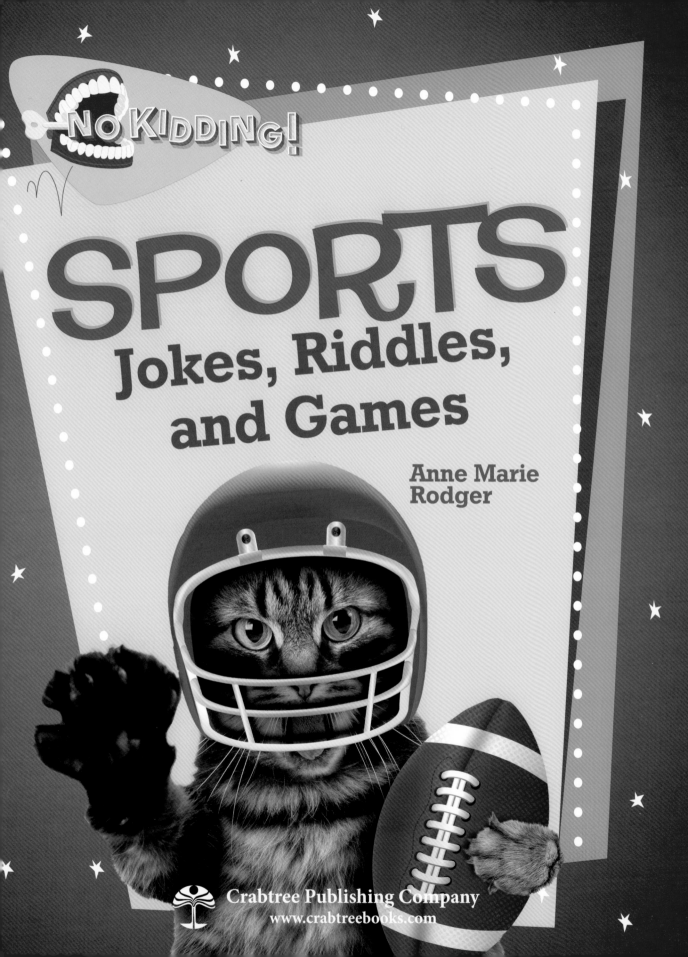

NO KIDDING!

SPORTS
Jokes, Riddles, and Games

Anne Marie Rodger

Crabtree Publishing Company
www.crabtreebooks.com

Crabtree Publishing Company
www.crabtreebooks.com

Author: Anne-Marie Rodger

Editorial Director: Ellen Rodger

Art Director: Rosie Gowsell Pattison

Editor: Petrice Custance

Proofreader: Janine Deschenes

Prepress technician: Margaret Amy Salter

Print and production coordinator: Katherine Berti

Production coordinated by Plan B Book Packagers

Photographs:
Cover/title page: Foto Yakov/Shutterstock; p.3: DJ Taylor/Shutterstock; p.4: Hit Toon.Com/Shutterstock; p.5 (LOLE): Pushkin/Shutterstock; p.5 (UPRT): Ded Mazay/Shutterstock; p.6: Angkrit/Shutterstock; p.8 (LOLE): Danilo Sanino/Shutterstock; p. 8 (LORT), Africa Studio/Shutterstock; p.10 (LOLE): Eric Isselee/Shutterstock; p.10 (UPRT): Fongman/Shutterstock; p.11 (LOLE): Glyph Stock/Shutterstock; p.11 (UPRT): Annette Shaff/Shutterstock; p.12: Elnur/Shutterstock; p.13: Laszlo Szirtesi/Shutterstock; p.14: Elnur/Shutterstock; p.15 (UP): Mike Elliott/Shutterstock; p.15 (LOLE): Ivan Nikulin/Shutterstock; p.16: Andrey Makurin; p.17 (LOLE): Javier Brosch/Shutterstock; p.17 (UPRT): Indigo Fish/Shutterstock; p.18: Stefano Moscardini/Shutterstock; p.19 (LOLE): Rene Ramos/Shutterstock; p.19 (UPRT): Igor Kovalchuk; p.20: Stock Creations/Shutterstock; p. 21 (LOLE): Duplass; p.21 (UPRT): Anton Batov/Shutterstock; p.22: Blue Ring Media/Shutterstock; p.23 (LOLE): PathDoc/Shutterstock; p.23 (UPRT): Ron Leishman/Shutterstock; p.24: Lorelyn Medina/Shutterstock; p.25 (LOLE): Lisa F. Young/Shutterstock; p.25 (UPRT): Rashevskyi Viacheslav/Shutterstock; p.26: Javier Brosch/Shutterstock; p.27: Ron Leishman/Shutterstock; p.28: Kenny K./Shutterstock; p.29: Karelin 621/Shutterstock; p.30: Willee Cole Photography/Shutterstock; p.31: Joe Seer/Shutterstock; p.31: Ga Fullner/Shutterstock

Library and Archives Canada Cataloguing in Publication

Rodger, Anne-Marie, author
      Sports jokes, riddles, and games / Anne-Marie Rodger.

(No kidding!)
Includes index.
Issued in print and electronic formats.
ISBN 978-0-7787-2390-5 (bound).--
ISBN 978-0-7787-2394-3 (paperback).--
ISBN 978-1-4271-1747-2 (html)

      1. Sports--Juvenile humor. 2. Wit and humor, Juvenile. 3. Riddles, Juvenile. I. Title.

PN6231.S65R64 2016   jC818'.602   C2015-907481-9
                                                C2015-907482-7

Library of Congress Cataloging-in-Publication Data

Names: Rodger, Anne-Marie, author.
Title: Sports jokes, riddles, and games / Anne-Marie Rodger.
Description: New York : Crabtree Publishing, 2016. | Series: No Kidding! | Includes index.
Identifiers: LCCN 2016002544 (print) | LCCN 2016006082 (ebook) | ISBN 9780778723905 (reinforced library binding : alk. paper) | ISBN 9780778723943 (pbk. : alk. paper) | ISBN 9781427117472 (electronic HTML)
Subjects: LCSH: Sports--Juvenile humor. | Wit and humor, Juvenile.
Classification: LCC PN6231.S65 R54 2016 (print) | LCC PN6231.S65 (ebook) | DDC 808.88/2--dc23
LC record available at http://lccn.loc.gov/2016002544

Crabtree Publishing Company
www.crabtreebooks.com   1-800-387-7650

Printed in Canada/032016/EF20160210

Published in Canada
Crabtree Publishing
616 Welland Ave.
St. Catharines, Ontario
L2M 5V6

Published in the United States
Crabtree Publishing
PMB 59051
350 Fifth Avenue, 59th Floor
New York, New York 10118

Published in the United Kingdom
Crabtree Publishing
Maritime House
Basin Road North, Hove
BN41 1WR

Published in Australia
Crabtree Publishing
3 Charles Street
Coburg North
VIC, 3058

CONTENTS

CHAPTER I
OUTTA LEFT FIELD

What comes to mind when you think about sports? For some, it might be uniforms. Others might think of physical fitness or their favorite team mascot. But what about humor and making people laugh? Sports are serious, but they are also fun. And they can be really funny to watch. Think about the last time you saw a sports blooper reel on television. It may not be funny for the player who makes a mistake and slams into his teammate on the field, but it sure gets the viewer giggling!

Q **Why did the golfer wear two pairs of pants?**

A In case he got a hole in one.

HUMOR EASES TENSION

One of the reasons sports are such an easy subject for humor and jokes is that they can be very serious and tense. You may think its just a game, but try telling that to a professional player or coach! Laughing and joking helps people relax and takes the pressure off. It's also one way to make sense of the world around us. Why do we laugh or "make fun" when we see an athlete run, trip, and bounce back up again? One reason is because running seems so natural that a baby can do it. For a trained athlete, running shouldn't involve falling. Mistakes, especially **exaggerated** ones, can seem funny. But it's also important to understand when something is funny and when it's not. An athlete carried off the field on a stretcher is not something to laugh at.

HOW DOES A JOKE WORK?

QUESTION:
Why did Tarzan
spend so much time
on the golf course?

ANSWER:
He was perfecting
his swing!

See what we did here? In order to make
a joke that people will understand and find
humorous, we have to understand all of
the pieces of the joke and how they work together. For example, we
know that in the game of golf, you swing a golf club. We also know
that the character Tarzan lived in the jungle and liked to swing from
tree to tree. We are using the word "swing" but in reference to two
different things! In this case, swing is a homonym, a word that is
spelled and pronounced the same but has different meanings. In
the question, we **imply** club swinging, and in the answer we mean
swinging from tree to tree. Humor and joke-making are actually
very **complex** when you think about it. You have to understand how
language is used, and the culture of the
world around you.

Q Why did Cinderella get kicked
off the baseball team?

A Because she is
always running away
from the ball.

FUNNY BONE:
When a group of people are
lively and playing rough,
people typically refer to
that as *horseplay*. The
word is often used as a
metaphor for something
that is silly. *That's just
horseplay!*

What's a vampire's favorite sport?

Casket ball.

JOKE PARTS

So what exactly makes up a joke? How do you put one together? A joke really has two main parts:

The **Setup** and the **Punch Line.** The setup of a joke is the beginning, when you give your audience the **context**, or the background information, needed to get the joke.

For example, the question "what lights up a soccer stadium?" is a setup, since it tells the audience the **premise**, or the subject, of the joke. In this case, the premise is the game of soccer.

The punch line is the end of the joke, or the part that makes the audience laugh. A good joke usually works because the audience is taken in a surprising or unexpected direction. For example:

THE SETUP:
What lights up a soccer stadium?

THE PUNCH LINE:
A soccer match!

This punch line is a play on words. It takes the word match and humorously uses its two different meanings: match as in a soccer game, and match as in the wooden stick you strike to make a fire and create light. Wordplay includes the use of homonyms, homophones, or homographs. These are words that sound alike, or are spelled alike, but have different meanings.

Q **What position does a monster play on a soccer team?**

A Ghoulie.

HOMONYM WORDS

Sound the same, and can have the same or different spelling

Match *(a contest or game)*

Match *(something you strike to light a fire)*

Be *(to exist)*
Bee *(an insect)*

HOMOPHONE WORDS

Sound the same but have different spelling

Sell *(to exchange something for money)*

Cell *(a small room, and also, a microscopic unit or life form)*

Pare *(to cut away the edge of something)*

Pair *(two of any one thing)*

Pear *(a fruit)*

HOMOGRAPH OR HETERONYM WORDS

Sound the same or sound different, but have the same spelling

Lie *(to lie down horizontally)*

Lie *(to tell an untruth)*

Heteronym (Different sound but same spelling)

Tear *(a drop of water from the eye)*

Tear *(to rip something)*

FUNNY BONE:

Not all jokes are simple. Many are long or complicated and involve buildup, which is the creation of anticipation in a joke. It is important for the delivery of the joke, or how you tell it to the audience. Buildup keeps the audience interested, and eager to hear the joke's punch line.

CHAPTER 2
JUST PLAYING WITH YA!

Did you know that there are many different kinds of humor?

You are probably most familiar with one-liner jokes, but there are actually many different forms of humor. Read on and discover new ways to be the class clown.

FIDDLE WITH A RIDDLE

A riddle is a head-scratching question. Riddles require the audience to use their knowledge of language and the world around them to guess the answer. They typically use opposing **descriptors** to throw off the guesses. Riddles are often clever and funny.

For example, to arrive at the answer to the riddle on the left, you have to know that running makes you huff and puff!

PUNNING WITH YOU

A pun is a play on words, and you will often find one in a joke. A word can have multiple meanings, and a pun plays on those different meanings to create a humorous punch line. Puns also include different words that sound the same but have different meanings, like homophones or homographs, which can also get a chuckle.

How is the word batter used in this joke?

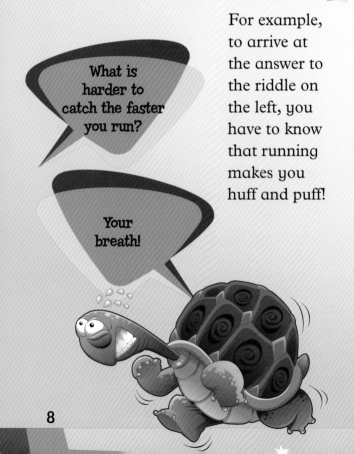

What is harder to catch the faster you run?

Your breath!

How is a baseball team similar to a pancake?

They both need a good batter!

HELP! I'M GAGGING!

A gag is a short, amusing story or scene. Visual gags are made of anything that presents humor visually instead of using words. These may include something unexpected happening, such as someone jumping out in front of a person to surprise them. In movie or television comedy, gag reels, also called blooper reels, are a collection of scenes showing unexpected and often hilarious mistakes.

IMITATION IS FLATTERY

Have you ever tried to **imitate** someone using exaggerated actions? You might have spoofed your mom, a sibling, or a friend by using their tone of voice or characteristic actions. If you have, you've performed a parody! Parody is humor that imitates, copies, or makes fun of someone or something in a comical way. For example, you can make a parody about a song by keeping the same melody and then swapping the lyrics with humorous ones. Parodies are also called spoofs, lampoons, or send-ups. What clever ones do you have up your sleeve?

Q Why did the soccer ball quit playing?

A It was tired of being kicked around.

FUNNY BONE:

Are fumbles funny? They can be! The word fumble means to be clumsy when handling something. It is typically used in sports when we see a player make a mistake, such as dropping a football. In comedy, to say that someone fumbled a joke means it was poorly delivered.

WHAT IS THIS LAUGHTER THING?

What is laughter? The question itself sounds silly. But it is worth looking at. Laughter is a collection of happy sounds that we make when we find something funny, or when we're just in normal social situations. You've done it **unconsciously** several times a day, ever since you were a baby. And you aren't the only one. Studies show that some animals, such as chimps, appear to laugh, especially when they are tickled.

Q What stroke do chickens swim?

A The breast stroke.

Q Why is it so loud at tennis matches?

A Because players raise such a racket.

WHAT HAPPENS WHEN WE LAUGH?

There is a lot that we do not know about laughter and the human body, but we do know that laughter is like exercise. It's good for us! Studies show (yes, laughter has been studied by scientists) that when we find something funny, a message is sent to our brain. Our brain then releases hormones and other chemicals throughout our body, making us feel happy. Laughter increases our ability to cope with and endure pain. It boosts our **immune system** and helps us fight disease. It also lowers stress, and protects our hearts by improving blood flow. What a great reason to get giggling!

Q What did the baseball glove say to the ball?

A Catch you later!

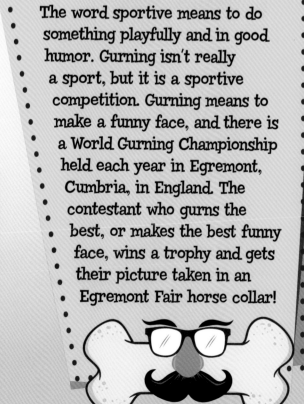

FUNNY BONE:

The word sportive means to do something playfully and in good humor. Gurning isn't really a sport, but it is a sportive competition. Gurning means to make a funny face, and there is a World Gurning Championship held each year in Egremont, Cumbria, in England. The contestant who gurns the best, or makes the best funny face, wins a trophy and gets their picture taken in an Egremont Fair horse collar!

CHAPTER 3
THE LANGUAGE OF HUMOR

Comedians and comics are masters of humor. They entertain crowds with their jokes, gags, and stories. They say funny things and act in funny ways. Most importantly, comedians and comics have a way of understanding language and culture in the world.

A HISTORY OF GUFFAWS

Comedy has a long history. It's at least as old as recorded time. Many ancient cultures appreciated humor. In ancient Greece, the author Aristophanes was known for his many comedies. Roman playwright Plautus wrote farces, which are comedies that use a lot of horseplay and unlikely situations. Plautus **influenced** William Shakespeare, a well-known English playwright from the late 1500s. Shakespeare's comedy plays use slapstick, puns, and other wordplay. They tell stories about the world and make fun of the wealthy and powerful.

DID YOU HEAR THE ONE ABOUT…

Comedians are some of our favorite entertainers both on television and in the movies. People even pay to see stand-up comedians at comedy clubs and events. Stand-up comedy is a form of comedy where a comedian performs jokes in front of a live audience. Telling jokes for a living is fun, but it is very difficult. Comedians can get **heckled**, or rudely interrupted, during shows. They often deal with hecklers by making fun of them.

Ancient Greek actors wore comedy masks while performing.

Q

Why is the Hockey Hall of Fame located in Toronto?

A It's the only way Leafs fans can see the Stanley Cup.

SPORTS COMEDY

Audiences love sports comedy, whether in movies or in real life. One reason for this might be the screwball comedy element that makes fun of the seriousness of sport. The Harlem Globetrotters is an exhibition basketball team that uses slapstick-style physical comedy to entertain. Of course, all of the team's players are highly-skilled athletes and the buffoonery highlights their skills. In fact, several National Basketball Association (NBA) players, including Wilt Chamberlain and Meadowlark Lemon, have been Globetrotters.

Harlem Globetrotters entertain crowds all over the world.

Q What do you call a New York Knicks player with a championship ring?

A A senior citizen.

HUMOR HEALS A LOSS

Sports humor often involves making fun of a team when it isn't playing well. The humor can border on mean, but it usually comes from the disappointment fans feel when their team loses. Consider the following joke that is often told by fans of losing teams. "A man's dying wish was that players from his favorite team act as **pallbearers** at his funeral. He wanted them to let him down one last time." Get it? "Let down" means a pallbearer's job of lowering a casket into the ground for burial, as well as the sadness a fan feels when their team loses.

FUNNY BONE:

Beginner's luck refers to when someone achieves something easily on the first try (like when you sink a putt the first time you golf!). This expression is commonly used by comedians if a beginner has an outstanding first show, and it's usually used dismissively. "The audience laughed at all your jokes? Eh, beginner's luck!"

SOUNDS SO SIMILE

A simile is when you compare two things that don't
normally go together in order to create an interesting
or funny description of something. Similes use
connecting words such as "like" or "as" to make these
comparisons. A lot of good humor uses similes because
they are easy to picture, and they can pack a punch
like a heavyweight boxing champion. Pack a punch...
heavyweight boxing champion...see what we did there?

THE ELEMENT OF SURPRISE

When comedians use similes, they typically do so
in extreme or surprising ways, which highlights how
silly the comparison is...and hopefully gets a
chuckle from the audience. For example:

The ballerina rose
gracefully en pointe and
extended one slender
leg behind her, like
a dog at a fire
hydrant.

Or how about:

See how these similes work?
They take two very normal
subjects—a ballerina's extended
leg and a goal keeper's hair—and
compare them with something
totally unexpected!

The goal keeper's
hair glistened in the
rain like a nose hair
after a sneeze.

Q What was the football coach doing at the parking meter?

A Trying to get his quarter back.

Q Why did your teacher put his toe in the water?

A He wanted to test it.

FUNNY BONE:

A mascot is the representative, or face, of a sports team. Mascots tend to be silly and they are often seen at sports games, exciting the crowd and doing funny tricks. Mascots typically don't speak. Their humor is all physical. What do you expect from a guy in a giant stuffed bear costume?

CHAPTER 4
WORD GAMES

Ah sports...the perfect forum for metaphors. Check this out:

Sports commentators are famous for their idioms. They really come out swinging and put on the full-court press when describing games and matches. But that's their **gambit**, because when it comes down to the wire, they are heavy hitters in the metaphor and idiom game. (That's called a slam dunk.)

FIGURE OF SPEECH OR WORDS TO LIVE BY?

Metaphors are figures of speech that are tailor-made for sports. Metaphors describe something by comparing it to something unrelated in order to highlight how the two things are alike. If that sounds confusing, just think of it this way:

"My birthday party is going to be so much fun. Mom has all the bases loaded!"

A birthday party can be compared to a baseball game with all the bases loaded. The term "bases are loaded" is used as a metaphor for being ready and prepared to score.

Q How do baseball players stay cool?

They sit next to their fans.

A

METAPHORS IN HUMOR

Metaphors can be a comedian's best friend. Using them is a clever way to put some smiles on faces. For example:

> The young fighter had a hungry look, the kind you get from not eating for a while.

Do you see the humor? Here, the hungry look is used as a metaphor for being competitive in a sport, while the description is quite literal, meaning the fighter is hungry for food. The comparison is unexpected, and because of that, it's funny!

Q What do you get when you run in front of a car?

A Tired.

FUNNY BONE:

Bit is a word that describes a small act or performance. This term is often used in humor because different jokes and stories tend to be short. For example, "Oh man, he's doing his angry baseball catcher bit."

17

I'M SUCH AN IDIOM!

Idioms usually go hand in hand with metaphors. Idioms are expressions or phrases whose words have different meanings than they **imply**, or seem to mean. Idioms have a figurative meaning that is not literal, or real. They also have a literal meaning that is actual, or true. If that sounds confusing, think of it this way, if someone says "that game is in the bag" they don't mean they have put the game inside a bag. They mean the game is easily won. If they say scoring a goal will be a "piece of cake" they don't mean it will be a tasty dessert. They mean it will be easy.

IDIOMS AND CULTURE

Idioms can be tricky to follow in a different language. That's because each language has its own expressions that are rooted deeply in the history and culture of a country. Take the Arabic language idiom "I don't have a camel in the caravan." It means "this isn't my business or concern," or "I don't have an interest in what happens." Camels and caravans are common in Arab culture and history, so it makes sense that the idiom would reflect this. In English, a similar idiom might be "I don't have a horse in this race."

Q Why did the chicken get a penalty during the soccer game?

A For fowl play.

SPORTS IDIOMS AND HUMOR

Idioms are a little bit like inside jokes that everyone tells. Everyone knows them and everyone uses them. That's what makes them funny. Of course, some idioms are funnier than others. Check out these other examples of sports idioms and their meanings:

I gave it my best shot (I gave it a try)

That opened up a can of worms
(caused a difficult or complicated problem)

The ball is in your court
(you have the responsibility)

It came down to the wire
(a close decision made at the last moment)

See how these idioms work? They take figurative language (best shot, can of worms, court) to describe something literal, such as giving something a try, or taking responsibility. A metaphor compares two unrelated subjects as a way of describing something. An idiom is an expression where the meaning is different than the literal meaning of the words used. Can you come up with more sports idioms?

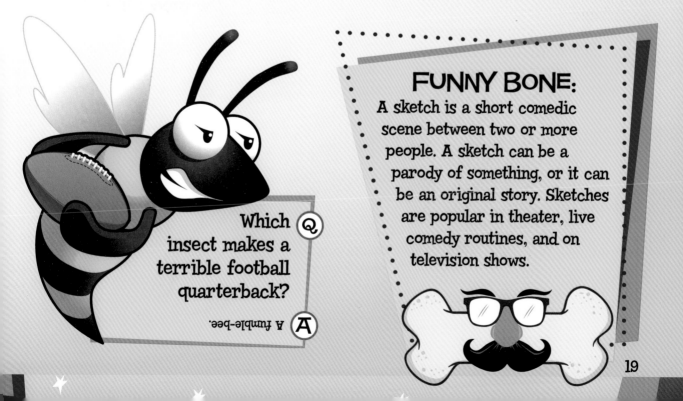

Q Which insect makes a terrible football quarterback?

A A fumble-bee.

FUNNY BONE:

A sketch is a short comedic scene between two or more people. A sketch can be a parody of something, or it can be an original story. Sketches are popular in theater, live comedy routines, and on television shows.

CHAPTER 5
GAFFES AND GIGGLES

One of the tricks to writing a good joke or a humorous story is to be inventive with the words and language you are using. You want to "shake it up" a little so that your story is interesting. That's where synonyms and antonyms come in handy.

DIFFERENT WORD, SAME MEANING

What's the old saying? That Inuit people have 100 words for snow? Well, actually they don't, but if they did, they would be called synonyms. A synonym is simply a word that has the same meaning as another word. You use them everyday. For example, when telling a story about a soccer game, you might use the word run. You might also use other words in place of run that mean the same thing, such as sprint, race, dart, fly, scurry, or charge. These words, while different, all describe a similar thing.

You can shake up humor with unexpected images as well.

SYNONYMOUS MOMENT

When we use synonyms in speech, we often use them to describe a particular moment. This gives our audience a clear picture. For example, instead of saying, "I ran down the field to score the winning goal" you might say, "I flew down the field to score the winning goal." This works because when we use a more descriptive synonym for the word ran, we are creating a more exciting account of the moment.

It's the same with humor. The more words we have to describe something, the more interesting and lively our story or joke will be. Humor is about being inventive, and the words we choose to use is a large part of that.

Q What is a runner's best subject in school?

A Jog-raphy.

Q Why do babies make great basketball players?

A Because they are always dribbling.

FUNNY BONE:

Slapstick is a type of humor which uses exaggerated physical comedy, such as falls and fake slaps, to get guffaws. The word slapstick comes from an Italian word for baton, or prop stick. The sticks were used in plays and made a loud sound when one actor would hit the other with it.

OPPOSITES ATTRACT

So synonym means using a different word with the same meaning. What about antonym? An antonym means a word that has the opposite meaning. For example, some possible antonyms of the word run are crawl, lag, stand, and dally. Understanding words and their meanings, as well as their opposite meanings, is an important element in wordplay, and it's the secret weapon of every comedian.

SNEAKY HUMOR

Everybody has at least one friend whose sense of humor is biting and sharp. When they joke, they really tear into their subject matter by saying the opposite of what they mean. This form of humor is called **sarcasm**. Sarcasm, when done well, can be very funny. But it can also be hurtful and offend people. Note to readers: sarcasm is particularly annoying to parents who are more likely to send you to your room for being rude than congratulate you for being shockingly clever with your jokes and jabs.

Q What is the hardest part about skydiving?

A The ground!

SARCASM WITHOUT SNEERING

There are ways to use sarcasm effectively, and it requires knowing your antonyms. For example, if your favorite team lost a big game, you might express your disappointment by saying, "Oh yeah, our goalie was just fantastic today, he really was an invisible force field." Sarcasm is best understood and interpreted in person, as the tone of voice is just as important as the words used. And if someone takes it the wrong way, you might be able to explain that you were just practicing your antonyms.

Be careful with sarcasm. It can easily be mistaken for nasty behavior.

Q What happened to the runner who had a fear of hurdles?

A He got over it.

FUNNY BONE:

When you're in the middle of telling a joke or funny story and pause for effect, it's called a beat. A beat is used for comedic timing and to keep your audience interested. You don't want to give the punch line away too fast!

CHAPTER 6
SPORTS FUN AND GAMES

Question: what do a hockey player and a magician have in common? Answer: they both do hat tricks! Haha. Did you get the joke? If so, why? Probably because you understand that a popular trick for a magician is to pull a rabbit out of a hat, and that a hat trick in the game of hockey is when a player scores three goals in one game. But what if you didn't get it? Understanding jokes about things such as sports are very specific to the immediate world around us, as well as the culture we belong to. If you had never heard of ice hockey before, you wouldn't understand the humor.

TENSION AND HUMOR

Sports can be both serious and funny. This natural tension can make silly mistakes and physical humor a relief. It's important to note that when we make jokes and laugh at sports or athletes, that we do it in a respectful way. Often, fans of certain teams or athletes can get frustrated with the outcome of a game or a season and may resort to making fun of that team or person. Professional athletes can take a little bit of ribbing. They've been trained to accept loss and failure as well as victory. It is different for amateur and younger athletes. Humor should not be personal or cruel about someone's mistakes. It is a fine line between having a good laugh and being nasty and hurtful.

Q Why did the pig drop out of the marathon?

A It pulled a hamstring.

24

FUNNY FANS

Have you ever been to a sporting event where the crowd is as entertaining as the game? Some sports are known for their wacky fans. In North America, professional and college football fans sometimes wear funny hats or paint their faces to show their devotion to their team. Some even paint their stomachs and go shirtless in freezing cold weather as a mark of their enthusiasm. Team mascots are meant to get crowds excited about the game. Mascots wear imaginative costumes. The best mascots also do funny dances or have **mock** arguments. Some even have giggle-worthy names such as Clawed Z. Eagle (American University in Washington, D.C.), YoUDee the Blue Hen (University of Delaware), or Gnarlz and Wild E. Cat (University of New Hampshire).

Q How do chickens show support for their favorite team?

A They egg them on!

GO TEAM

FUNNY BONE:

Have you ever made a flop or been a flop? Flopping is an entertainment term that describes how a comedian's act bombs, or fails to get a laugh. It can also describe a play or movie that doesn't attract an audience. It brings to mind a picture of a fish flopping around helplessly on land.

MATCH THE METAPHORS AND IDIOMS

Have you ever watched professional players or coaches being interviewed after a game? If there's one thing they excel at off the field, it's metaphors and idioms. Ask them how the game went and they'll say "we gave 110 percent," or "it's not a sprint, it's a marathon." You have to be an expert in idiomology to know what they are saying! Try your hand at matching these idioms to their meanings:

MATCHING GAME

1. Drop the ball

2. Sucker punch

3. Drop the gloves

4. Down and out

5. Up to par

A. An unexpected blow (boxing)
Remember that time your best friend blamed you for the lunchtime macaroni and cheese explosion of 2012? You got detention for a week!

B. Being unlucky; not having very much
Have you ever felt sad and not have any interest in hanging out or doing the things you like, such as stamp-collecting or fire-eating?

C. To engage in a confrontation
Think of a time you were really upset and wanted to confront someone, like when your little sister flushed all of your markers down the toilet!

D. To make an error (baseball)
Remember that time that you forgot to hang up your aunt's laundry and put it in the dryer instead? Now she has a great wardrobe for dolls!

E. To meet (or not) expectations
How about that time when you were really excited for mom's apple pie? You thought it was better than great!

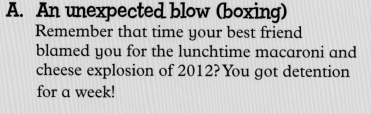

Answers: 1.D, 2.A, 3.C, 4.B, 5.E

THAT'S WACKY TALK!

If you were an alien and landed on Planet Sports, the language would be very confusing. It's confusing for mere Earthlings! Each sport has its own funny insider slang. You would need a sports dictionary to know them all. How many of these can you put in a sentence? Do you have any of your own to add?

Deke
–to move around your opponent like in soccer or hockey!

Sacked
–when the quarterback gets tackled to the ground in football!

Nutmegged
–in soccer, when you **maneuver** the ball between the opposite players legs!

Split the Uprights
–when you score a field goal in football

Sticky Wicket
–A wet and soggy field in the game of cricket

Q Why do horse jockeys have such a bad reputation?

A Because they like to stirrup trouble.

FUNNY BONE:
You know that joke that comes up multiple times throughout a comedy show or comedic story, but in different ways? It's got a name, and it's called a running gag. A running gag could be something like how your family is always joking about your dad's cooking or your brother's smelly socks.

CHAPTER 7
HOW TO BE FUNNY

Learning to be funny is like learning to cook or ride a bike. With the right tools and knowledge, you'll be well on your way to being the funniest person this side of the tennis court! We'll show you how...

FUNNY 101

Telling jokes can be an exercise in memory management. Here are some tips to memorizing jokes so that you hit it out of the park every time!

1. **Memorize the punch line.** Jokes are all about the unexpected. If you get halfway through the joke and forget the clever punch line, oh no! Memorizing the funniest part of the joke is a great place to start.

2. **Practice Practice Practice.** The more you practice a joke and its delivery, the better you'll do every time! Use friends and family as a sounding board.

3. **Visualize.** Do you ever find it's easier to remember things if you have a personal connection to them? Try it with a joke! Set the joke in your favorite place and then picture it in your mind. Easy-peasy!

4. **Be physical.** Think of yourself as an actor on a stage. Many actors find it easier to remember lines when they have certain movements, such as walking back and forth, connected to their lines. Practice your joke with hand gestures to help you memorize it!

5. **Write your jokes down.** All of the great comedians write their material down. This way you'll have a record of your jokes to refer to whenever you want.

MAKE YOUR OWN BASEBALL CARD

Have you ever owned or collected player cards? How about making your own? You'll need:

1. **A funny picture of the athlete you are profiling.** This can be you, a friend, or even a made-up character from a made-up sport! Place the picture on a piece of thick paper or cardboard, and then cut into a 2 ½ inch by 3 ½ inch (6.4 cm by 8.9 cm) rectangle.

2. **Lots of athletes have cool nicknames.** Get creative and think of a funny one! Eugene "The Giggler" Hornswaggle and April "Last Month" Schenk are two of our favorites.

3. **Include some statistics on their career on the back of the card.** In order for the card to seem very silly and over the top, make up some crazy stats! For example: "Hornswaggle can stuff 200 marshmallows into his mouth," or "April once played a whole game with her underwear on backwards!"

4. **Create a brief biography.** Many athlete playing cards include a brief **biography**. Think of a funny backstory, for example: "Eugene made the team after hitting home runs using nothing but a toilet brush and a smile."

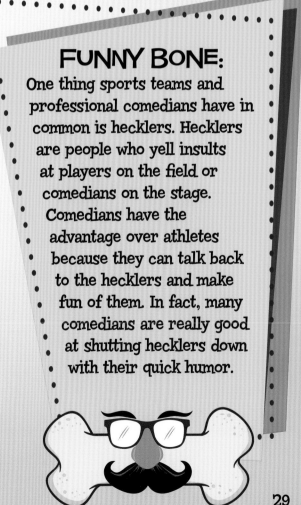

FUNNY BONE:
One thing sports teams and professional comedians have in common is hecklers. Hecklers are people who yell insults at players on the field or comedians on the stage. Comedians have the advantage over athletes because they can talk back to the hecklers and make fun of them. In fact, many comedians are really good at shutting hecklers down with their quick humor.

BULLSEYE

HORNSWAGGLE

CHAPTER 8
FIND OUT MORE

Loving the humor game? Can't get enough? For more joke ideas, tips, and information on all things funny, check out these sources.

BOOKS:

Korman, Gordon. *The Toilet Paper Tigers*. Apple Paperbacks, 1995.

Leno, Jay. *How to Be the Funniest Kid in the Whole Wide World.* Simon & Schuster, 2005.

Stabler, David. *Kid Athletes: True Tales of Childhood from Sports Legends.* Quirk Books, 2015.

WEBSITES:

www.sikids.com/games
This Sports Illustrated site for kids includes all kinds of sports-related fun and games.

http://funkidsjokes.com/kids-jokes/kids-sports-jokes/
This website has enough sports jokes and riddles to make you a champ!

HALL OF HUMOR

Yogi Berra

Yogi Berra was a baseball superstar in the 1940s and 1950s. He was well known for his **malapropisms,** where one word is mistakenly used for another similar-sounding one. Some of his famous slips included:

This is like déjà-vu all over again
(The joke being that déjà-vu is a term for experiencing something more than once!)

You can observe a lot just by watching
(This probably explains itself.)

Baseball is 90 percent mental— the other half is physical
(Hopefully this one does too...)

Shaquille O'Neal

"Shaq" is a famous basketball star who is as well-known for his sense of humor as for his size. He's over seven feet (2.1 m) tall! Shaq played in the National Basketball Association and retired in 2011 after 19 years as a professional athlete. He likes to make jokes and be silly. He's also known for his witty banter and tongue-in-cheek statements, such as:

I'm tired of hearing about money, money, money. I just want to play the game, drink Pepsi, and wear Reebok.
(This is a funny quote because he says he doesn't care about making money, but mentions some sponsors who pay him a lot of money to use their products!)

If I were a painter, you'd call me Shaqcasso.
(Here he humbly compares his basketball skills to those of the famous artist Pablo Picasso.)

GLOSSARY

Note: Some boldfaced words are defined where they appear in the text.

biography A story of someone's life, their achievements, and their history

complex Complicated and difficult

descriptors Words that describe or identify something

exaggerated To make something bigger, better, scarier, or more important than it really is

gambit An action at the beginning of a game, where a risk is taken to gain an advantage

imitate To copy, echo, or parrot someone or something

imply To strongly suggest something through hinting instead of saying it directly

immune system The body's system for fighting off disease

influenced To have an effect on something, or to shape or change something

maneuver A planned action to steer or move something in a specific direction

mock To ridicule or make fun of something; also something that is fake or not real

pallbearer A person who helps carry a coffin at a funeral

unconsciously Something you are not conscious or aware of doing or feeling

INDEX